Prayers *for* Reflection

David Adam
Nick Fawcett
Gerald O'Mahony
Susan Sayers
Ray Simpson

Compiled by Sue Cowper

www.kevinmayhew.com

Prayers compiled from:

1000 Prayers for Public Worship – David Adam
2000 Prayers for Public Worship – Nick Fawcett
A Thousand and One Prayers – Gerald O'Mahony
1500 Prayers for Public Worship – Susan Sayers
His Complete Celtic Prayers – Ray Simpson

 KM PUBLISHING

First published in Great Britain in 2013 by Kevin Mayhew Ltd
Buxhall, Stowmarket, Suffolk IP14 3BW
Tel: +44 (0) 1449 737978 Fax: +44 (0) 1449 737834
E-mail: info@kevinmayhew.com

www.kevinmayhew.com

9 8 7 6 5 4 3 2 1 0

ISBN 978 1 84867 660 2
Catalogue No. 1501408

Cover design by Rob Mortonson
© Images used under licence from Shutterstock Inc.
Typeset by Richard Weaver

Printed and bound in Great Britain

About the authors

DAVID ADAM was the Vicar of Lindisfarne, off the Northumbrian coast, for thirteen years until he retired in March 2003. His work involved ministering to thousands of pilgrims and other visitors. He is the author of many inspiring books on spirituality and prayer, and his Celtic writings have rekindled a keen interest in our Christian heritage.

NICK FAWCETT was brought up in Southend-on-Sea, Essex, and trained for the Baptist ministry at Bristol and Oxford, before serving churches in Lancashire and Cheltenham. He subsequently spent three years as a chaplain with the Christian movement Toc H, before focusing on writing and editing, which he continues with today, despite wrestling with cancer. He lives with his wife, Deborah, and two children – Samuel and Kate – in Wellington, Somerset, worshipping at the local Anglican church. A keen walker, he delights in the beauty of the Somerset and Devon countryside around his home, his numerous books owing much to the inspiration he unfailingly finds there.

GERALD O'MAHONY was born in Wigan, Lancashire. He joined the Society of Jesus (the Jesuits) at the age of 18, and was ordained priest aged 30. Gerald was a school teacher for four years, before being invited to join the team of advisers in religious education for the Archdiocese of Liverpool. Ten years on he joined another team, as retreat giver and writer in Loyola Hall Jesuit Spirituality Centre, Rainhill, near Liverpool, where he has lived and worked happily ever since. He is the author of twenty-four books, many of which have been published by Kevin Mayhew.

SUSAN SAYERS is the author of many popular resource books for the church. Through the conferences and workshops she is invited to lead, she has been privileged to share in the worship of many different traditions and cultures. A teacher by profession, she was ordained a priest in the Anglican Church and, before her retirement, her work was divided between the parish of Westcliff-on-Sea, the local women's prison, writing, training days and retreats.

RAY SIMPSON is a Celtic new monastic for tomorrow's world, a lecturer, consultant, liturgist, and author of some 30 books. He is the founding guardian of the international Community of Aidan and Hilda and the pioneer of its e-studies programmes. He is an ordained member of the Christian church and lives on the Holy Island of Lindisfarne. His website is www.raysimpson.org

1   Blessed are you, Lord our God.
    You never leave us or forsake us.
    You have promised us the victory
    through our Lord Jesus Christ.
    Lord, help us to know you and to trust in you always.
    Let us know that in you is the gift of life eternal
    and that through you we have the power
    to survive whatever happens to us or to the world.
    Blessed are you, God Almighty,
    Father, Son and Holy Spirit.   *David Adam*

2   Blessed are you, Lord our God,
    for you have sent your Son to be our Saviour.
    In the darkness of this world he comes to be our light.
    He has triumphed over pain and death
    and opened to us the way to everlasting life.
    He has revealed your love
    and made us sons and daughters of God.
    Blessed are you, Father, Son and Holy Spirit.   *David Adam*

3   Blessed are you, Lord God of our salvation.
    To you be praise and glory for ever.
    You have delivered us from the darkness of death
    through your beloved Son.
    In him, light has conquered darkness;
    life has triumphed over death.
    He has breathed into us your life-giving Spirit.
    Blessed are you, Father, Son and Holy Spirit,
    our God for ever and ever.   *David Adam*

4   Blessed are you, God and Father of us all,
    giver of life and life eternal.
    By the love of your Son you have triumphed over hatred.
    In his power, light has conquered darkness
    and life has overcome death.
    You have opened for us the gate of eternal life. *David Adam*

5 God of the desert,
   there you spoke to Moses,
   there you prepared John the Baptist;
   let us know that you are with us in the desert of doubt.
   When our feelings do not sense you,
   when our minds begin to question you,
   continue as our guardian and guide.
   Lead us out of our darkness into light,
   until we come out of the wilderness
   and share the joys of the Promised Land.   *David Adam*

6 We give thanks
   for all who have shared their faith with us
   and all who have witnessed to you
   in times of trouble.
   We ask your blessing
   upon all who are struggling with their faith at this time,
   all who are caught up with doubt
   or who are giving way to despair.
   May the light and love of Christ bring them new hope.
                                                  David Adam

7 We give thanks for your faithful people
   throughout the world,
   for the fellowship of all believers.
   We ask you to bless all who preach and teach
   the reality of the resurrection.
   We pray for all who are struggling with doubt
   and for all who are seeking a relationship with you.
                                                  David Adam

8 Lord,
   as we enter into the stillness, calm our hearts and
   our minds.
   Let all the storms within us cease, and enfold us in your peace.
   We come in weakness to you for strength;
   we come in our sinfulness for your forgiveness;
   we come wearied by life for your refreshing grace;
   we come out of our darkness to your love and light.
   Lord, renew, refresh, restore us by your presence and
   your power.   *David Adam*

9 Lord, in the stillness, speak to us;
   in the emptiness, come to us and fill us;
   to our troubles, come with your peace;
   to our weakness, come with your strength;
   in our doubts and our fears, abide with us.
   Still the storms within us and let us find rest in you.
   Help us to be the people you want us to be,
   and to achieve what you want us to do,
   that we may go out in confidence
   and serve you all our days.
   Through Jesus Christ our Lord, who is alive and reigns
   with you and the Holy Spirit, one God now and for ever.
   David Adam

10 God, we seek you until we find you.
    When we find you, help us to know you
    for when we know you, then we can love you.
    Help us to come before you
    through Jesus Christ our Lord.   *David Adam*

11 We come to you, dear Lord, as seekers;
    we are hungry for your love and your care.
    We ask you to bless all who are pilgrims and seekers,
    all who long for an awareness
    of your presence and your power.   *David Adam*

12 God of all love and beauty,
    open our hearts to welcome you,
    that your Son Jesus Christ, in his coming,
    may find us looking and longing for him
    and may find in us a dwelling prepared for himself:
    who is alive and reigns with you and the Holy Spirit,
    One God now and for ever.   *David Adam*

13 Blessed are you, Lord our God,
    in your love and care for your creation.
    You do not turn away any who come to you.
    You come to meet the seekers
    and provide refreshment for all who hunger and thirst.

You care for the broken and the fragmented
and want nothing to be lost.
Blessed are you, Father, Son and Holy Spirit.   *David Adam*

14   We give thanks that you seek and desire to save
     all who are lost or in the depths.
     We ask you to guide and bless
     all who are new to the faith,
     the newly converted, the baptised
     and the confirmed.
     Bless, O Lord, all who are seekers
     and those who are longing for a change in their lives.
                                                  David Adam

15   We pray for all who are seekers and pilgrims,
     all who search for the meaning of life and for purpose.
     We remember all who have lost touch with you
     or who have no faith.
     We pray for all who are caught up in materialism
     or who are self-centred.
     We ask that the Church may reach out
     to draw others to you.   *David Adam*

16   Lord, open our eyes to your presence:
     open our ears to your call.
     Open our lips to sing your praises.
     Open our hearts to your great love.
     May we awaken out of sleep
     that we may be aware of you,
     glimpse at your great glory
     and enjoy your presence.   *David Adam*

17   Lord, awaken us to your call.
     Open our ears to hear your words,
     open our eyes to your presence,
     open our hands with your generosity,
     open our hearts to your love,
     that we may live and work for you,
     Jesus Christ our Lord.   *David Adam*

18   Blessed are you, Lord our God,
     for you give us life and life eternal.
     You have given us the power to grow and to change.
     You have given us the freedom to ignore or turn to you.
     In your love you seek us
     and want us to have the fullness of life.   *David Adam*

19   Lord God,
     impart to us an adventurous spirit.
     We do not travel alone.
     Our God is with us.   *David Adam*

20   May the bright light of Christ enlighten our hearts,
     shine in our minds and direct our journeying,
     and give light to the world.   *David Adam*

21   God, you go with us on all our journeys.
     Protect us from all evil
     and keep us always in your love and your care.
     We ask your blessing
     upon all who are refugees or homeless.   *David Adam*

22   Blessed are you, Lord God,
     for you are with us in our journeying
     and in our resting.
     You are to be found in our homes
     and our daily lives.
     You, Lord, are our hope and our strength:
     in you we trust.   *David Adam*

23   Living God,
     we know our weakness all too well:
     our lack of faith,
     our limited courage,
     our flawed commitment.
     We know, should testing come,
     that we will struggle to hold on,
     our discipleship less secure than we would wish.

Protect us, then, from evil,
safeguard us from temptation,
and deliver us from times of trial,
through Jesus Christ our Lord.   *Nick Fawcett*

24 Lord of all,
open our hearts to others and to all you would say
through them,
and so open our hearts to you and to your life-giving word.
In Christ's name we ask it.   *Nick Fawcett*

25 Sovereign God,
whenever you speak,
teach us to listen;
whatever you ask,
teach us to respond;
wherever you lead,
teach us to follow;
however you work,
teach us to trust.
Give us a spirit of true meekness,
ready to give you pride of place in our life
and to offer you obedient and devoted service,
through Jesus Christ our Lord.   *Nick Fawcett*

26 Gracious God,
grant us an open mind,
a responsive heart and a receptive spirit,
that we might hear your voice,
however you choose to speak.   *Nick Fawcett*

27 Living God,
we would hear your voice, your word;
not ours or any other.
Speak now and help us to listen and respond,
in Jesus' name.   *Nick Fawcett*

28 Gracious God,
  for your call to be your people
  and your invitation to share in the work of your kingdom,
  we praise you.
  Help us to respond wholeheartedly
  and to live up to the trust you have placed in us,
  through Jesus Christ our Lord.   *Nick Fawcett*

29 Gracious God,
  give us strength to answer your call.
  May we be ready,
  like so many before us,
  to respond in faith and follow where you might lead,
  to the glory of your name.   *Nick Fawcett*

30 Living God,
  teach us to hear your cry in the groans of the hungry,
  the suffering of the sick,
  the plight of the homeless
  and the sorrow of the bereaved;
  to hear your call in the misery of the lonely,
  the despair of the oppressed,
  the plea of the weak
  and the helplessness of the poor.
  Teach us to listen and to respond,
  in the name of Christ.   *Nick Fawcett*

31 Sovereign God,
  you have called us to be your people:
  help us, then,
  to live as your children,
  to the glory of your name.   *Nick Fawcett*

32 Loving God,
  there are times in our lives
  when you call us to tasks that seem beyond us,
  tasks we would rather avoid.
  We hear your voice but feel unable to meet the challenge
  and our natural inclination is to run away.

Remind us that when you ask us to do something,
you give us the strength to do it.
Give us courage, then,
to respond when you call,
knowing that, however things may seem,
you are always able to transform them
in ways far beyond our expectations.   *Nick Fawcett*

33   Mighty God,
challenge us through the example of Jesus –
his humble acceptance of his calling
and his faithfulness to the last –
to consider our own calling:
to follow as his disciples,
his witnesses, his people.
Instruct, equip and inspire us,
that, by his grace,
we might show similar faithfulness and humility,
and honour the commitment we have made,
today and every day.   *Nick Fawcett*

34   Lord Jesus Christ,
we praise you today for your obedience to God's call,
your willingness to commit yourself
to the way of service, sacrifice and self-denial
so that we might become children of God.
Give us, as we worship you,
a clearer understanding of all that means –
the joy it offers and responsibility it entails –
so that we might commit ourselves more fully to you
and respond in turn to your call,
for your name's sake.   *Nick Fawcett*

35   Lord Jesus Christ,
help us today to hear again your call to discipleship,
and faithfully to follow wherever you would lead.
May the good news of your living, dying and rising
among us
resonate afresh deep within,

stirring us to sincere repentance,
deeper faith and renewed service.
Teach us now to live more authentically as your people,
in the light of your kingdom.   *Nick Fawcett*

36 Lord Jesus Christ,
Redeemer,
deliverer,
we remember today your obedience to God's call –
your readiness to commit your life
to the way of service and sacrifice,
surrendering yourself in order to save others.
Challenge us through that example
to consider our own faith and calling:
the nature of our discipleship
and the priorities we set in our lives.
Help us, remembering all you have done for us
and celebrating the love you continue so constantly to show,
to commit ourselves again to the growth of your kingdom
on earth as it is in heaven.   *Nick Fawcett*

37 Gracious God,
we thank you that you have spoken throughout history,
calling people to your service.
We thank you for those who have had the courage to respond,
even when that call has involved unpopularity,
ridicule and persecution.
We thank you that these were ordinary everyday people,
just like us:
hesitant, fearful,
uncertain of their ability to do what you asked of them,
yet receiving the strength they needed when they needed it.
Still today you call your people to challenging areas of service –
to jobs they would rather not do,
issues they would rather not face
and messages they would rather not deliver.
Yet, once again, you promise that you will give each one of
your people
the resources they need to meet the task.

Give us, then, courage to hear your voice
and to respond to your call,
through Jesus Christ our Lord.   *Nick Fawcett*

38   Living God,
we praise you that you have called us to faith in Christ,
to fellowship in your Church,
to Christian discipleship.
We praise you that you keep on calling us
to new avenues of service,
new ways of serving you,
new ways of working towards your kingdom.
Forgive us that we are sometimes slow or unwilling to respond:
we do not always understand what you are asking of us,
we resist when your call is too demanding,
we run from that which we would rather not do.
Thank you that though we ignore or disobey your call,
still you seek us out,
gently and lovingly leading us back to your way
and entrusting to us,
despite our faithlessness,
the message of the gospel.
Thank you for being a God full of mercy:
slow to anger,
abounding in steadfast love,
your nature always to forgive –
a God who is always ready to give a second chance,
repeatedly showing your patience,
demonstrating your awesome grace time and time again.
Help us to hear your voice clearly,
to accept your will humbly
and to respond to it gladly.
We ask it in the name of Christ.   *Nick Fawcett*

39   Lord,
you do not call us all to positions of eye-catching responsibility,
but we each have a part to play in your service nonetheless.
Whatever our gifts,
we have a contribution to make

that you can use in fulfilling something of your
eternal purpose.
Teach us, then, to listen for your voice,
and, when you call,
to respond gladly,
offering whatever you ask whenever you need it,
to the glory of your name.   *Nick Fawcett*

40   Loving God,
we thank you for your call:
to discipleship, fellowship and service;
to sharing as your people in the work of your kingdom.
We thank you that you call us as we are,
with all our faults, weaknesses and doubts,
accepting us not through our own deserving,
but through your grace,
your love,
and your mercy.
Above all, we thank you for the inner presence of your
Holy Spirit,
through which Christ is constantly at work within us,
moving deep within to change our lives
and to draw us ever closer to you.
Loving God,
receive our praise in his name.   *Nick Fawcett*

41   Lord Jesus Christ,
you speak your word to us
as you spoke it to the Apostles long ago:
'Come, follow me.'
You call us, as you have called so many over the years:
'Come to me,
all who are weary of carrying heavy burdens,
and I will give you rest.'
You offer us,
as you offer all your people,
refreshment for our souls,
promising that anyone who is thirsty can come to you
and drink.

Lord,
we thank you for that invitation,
and gladly we respond.
But, more than that, we thank you that before anyone
comes to you,
you come first to them.
You came to Peter, James and John by the lakeside;
to the hungry, the sick and the outcasts in the streets
of Galilee;
to Mary Magdalene weeping in the garden;
to two weary disciples walking the Emmaus Road;
to the Apostles trembling behind locked doors;
to Saul breathing murder on the road to Damascus;
and so to countless others since.
Always it is you who make the first approach,
calling your people to faith,
and still you come through your Spirit to meet with us.
Open our eyes to your presence
and lead us forward in your service until that day when,
with all your people,
we enter your kingdom and meet you face to face.
In your name we ask it.   *Nick Fawcett*

42   Gracious God,
     you act in ways we do not expect,
     you speak in ways we do not always understand,
     you come at times and in places we least imagine,
     and all too easily we fail to recognise your presence
     amongst us.
     Teach us to be awake to your prompting,
     however unlikely it may seem,
     and to respond whenever you call
     even though we have no idea where it might lead.
     Equip us to walk in faith,
     through Jesus Christ our Lord.   *Nick Fawcett*

43   Loving God,
     forgive us for refusing sometimes to listen to your voice.
     Deep down in our heart of hearts we know you are
     speaking to us,
     but we would rather not hear.

When your message is too demanding,
when you ask of us what we would rather not face,
when your words make us feel uncomfortable,
striking too near the mark,
we stubbornly resist,
closing our ears and pushing you away.
Yet however hard we may try,
we will never finally silence your voice –
not until we have listened and responded.
Help us, then, to hear what you would say to us,
and act upon it.
                                                    Nick Fawcett

44 Loving God,
there are times when,
no matter how we call,
you seem silent,
when we cannot hear your voice
no matter how we listen for it.
Grant us courage in those moments
to ask if we have closed our hearts and minds
to what you would say,
but help us also to understand that there are times
when you expect us to get on with the business of discipleship
without you directing our every step.
Help us to see that your silence need not be a sign of
our faithlessness
or of your displeasure,
but might rather point to your love,
offering us the opportunity to grow towards
Christian maturity.
Help us, then, to remember all those times you have spoken,
unmistakably,
to us
and to others,
and let those moments sustain and direct us
until your word comes again,
in the name of Christ.
                                                    Nick Fawcett

45   Almighty God,
teach us to build our life on the rock of faith,
the foundations of truth and the cornerstone of Christ,
each part cemented together by love.
So, through good or bad,
joy or sorrow,
pleasure or pain,
may we stand firm,
secure in the knowledge of your sovereign purpose
and saving grace.   *Nick Fawcett*

46   Gracious God,
may we not simply proclaim you as Lord,
nor simply worship you as such,
but may we also live each to your glory,
showing the sincerity of our commitment
through the depth of our love,
the extent of our service
and the pattern of our life,
to the glory of your name.   *Nick Fawcett*

47   Lord Jesus Christ,
teach us not just to proclaim you as the way,
the truth and the life,
but to follow you faithfully with total integrity,
and with everything we are,
so that our whole being speaks of you and for you,
to the glory of your name.   *Nick Fawcett*

48   Loving God,
teach us that asking for your name to be honoured is
not enough:
that, as well as words we must offer deeds –
a life that brings you glory
and that honours everything you stand for,
all you represent.
So, then, work within us until all we are,
think, say and do promotes your kingdom
and redounds to your honour,
through Jesus Christ our Lord.   *Nick Fawcett*

49 Mighty and mysterious God,
     we cannot answer for others
     but we will have to answer for ourselves.
     Teach us, then, to serve you faithfully,
     to love you truly, in word and deed,
     and to trust finally in your redeemed grace
     on which we all depend,
     through Jesus Christ our Lord.   *Nick Fawcett*

50 Sovereign God,
     save us from offering half-hearted discipleship,
     compromised commitment,
     divided loyalty,
     vacillating service.
     Teach us to offer all to you
     as surely as you offered your all to us in Christ.
     In his name we pray.   *Nick Fawcett*

51 Gracious God,
     when the spark of faith starts to flicker
     and the fire of commitment grows cold,
     rekindle in us the joy with which we first started out,
     so that we may awake each day with hope in our heart
     and live each moment rejoicing in your love,
     to the glory of your name.   *Nick Fawcett*

52 Gracious God,
     may our vision be clear,
     our commitment strong and our faith constant,
     and so may your light shine through us,
     to the glory of your name.   *Nick Fawcett*

53 Lord Jesus Christ,
     save us from simply knowing about you;
     help us truly to know you as our Lord,
     Saviour and friend,
     through your grace.   *Nick Fawcett*

54   Lord Jesus Christ,
     help us to follow in your footsteps,
     walking where you might lead us,
     trusting in your guidance.
     Teach us that wherever you ask us to go,
     you will be walking with us,
     matching us stride for stride.   *Nick Fawcett*

55   Almighty God,
     we commit to you not simply a part but all of life,
     asking that you will take who and what we are,
     and everything we do,
     and dedicate it to your service,
     for your name's sake.   *Nick Fawcett*

56   Gracious God,
     take our faith, flawed though it is,
     our love, poor though it may be,
     and our commitment, with all its imperfections,
     and use us in your service to make known your
     gracious purpose,
     through Jesus Christ our Lord.   *Nick Fawcett*

57   Lord Jesus Christ,
     we come to you in worship,
     seeking to learn more of you
     and to welcome you more fully into our lives.
     We come,
     yearning to love as you have loved us –
     to show the truth of our faith
     and the authenticity of our discipleship
     through our devotion to one another and to you,
     and through our concern for others.
     Help us, through this service,
     to recognise the ways in which we fall short of that calling,
     to acknowledge these honestly to you,
     and to open our hearts afresh to your grace,
     so that your love might grow within us
     and overflow to your praise and glory.   *Nick Fawcett*

58 Gracious God,
help us today to grasp more clearly
that it is in giving we receive,
in losing we find,
in sacrifice we find reward,
and in dying to self that we rise to new life.
In that knowledge, may we willingly accept the cost of
discipleship,
knowing that, whatever is asked of us,
the rewards of your kingdom are beyond price.
Open our eyes afresh today to that truth,
through Jesus Christ our Lord.   *Nick Fawcett*

59 Almighty God,
help us truly to worship you –
to offer not superficial show,
empty piety,
lifeless ritual
or outward observance,
but heartfelt praise,
true thanksgiving,
genuine penitence,
sacrificial commitment,
meaningful intercession
and a real hunger and thirst to know and serve you better.
Work within us now,
so that what we declare with our lips
we may believe in our hearts
and display in our lives,
to your glory.   *Nick Fawcett*

60 Lord Jesus Christ,
we believe you to be the way, the truth and the life,
but our faith is flawed and our commitment weak,
so that, all too easily and often, we go our own way,
losing sight of truth
and denying ourselves the fullness of life you offer.

Guide us now, as we worship,
so that we might walk with you more closely,
believe more truly,
and live more faithfully,
to the glory of God the Father.   *Nick Fawcett*

61   Lord Jesus Christ,
     we want to honour you by living as your disciples
     and walking in your way,
     but we find it hard,
     our inclinations so very different to your own.
     Reveal to us, we pray, more of what it means to follow you,
     more about the true nature of discipleship.
     Help us to grasp the meaning of your kingdom,
     where losers are winners,
     the first are last,
     and those who lose their life for your sake will truly find it.
     Teach us now,
     by your grace.   *Nick Fawcett*

62   Living God,
     reveal to us more of your will
     and equip us to honour it.
     Save us from taking the path of least resistance,
     opting for peace where there is no peace
     or pretending all is well when the reality is otherwise.
     Give us instead the faith and courage we need
     to stand up for what is right,
     even if that risks alienating people,
     including, perhaps, those we love.
     Hear us and help us, O God,
     in the name of Christ.   *Nick Fawcett*

63   Gracious God,
     we have committed ourselves to your service,
     but we are all too aware of how weak that commitment is
     and how often we fail to honour it.
     When our allegiance has been tested,
     our loyalty put on the line,

we have repeatedly been found wanting,
more concerned with our own interests than with
serving Christ.
When discipleship has involved cost,
and service meant putting ourselves out on behalf of others,
our good intentions have swiftly evaporated,
exposed as little more than fine-sounding ideas.
Gracious God,
we want to serve you better,
but we know that we will fail again,
just as we have failed before,
our faith flawed and our love imperfect.
Have mercy on us,
and through Christ's faithfulness to the last
inspire us to stay true to you
whatever life may bring.
For his name's sake we pray.   *Nick Fawcett*

64   Lord Jesus Christ,
we want to be true to our convictions,
to stand up for what is right,
but it's hard when the pressure is on.
It's hard not to bend when all around us disagree,
not to compromise for the sake of peace,
not to tone things down
when we find ourselves in the firing line.
Yet there are times when we need to stick our necks out
for what we believe in,
even when doing so may make us unpopular with others.
Give us wisdom to know when those times are,
and courage then to hold fast through them all.
                                                     Nick Fawcett

65   Lord Jesus Christ,
so often we let you down
because we are not serious about following you.
Afraid of what unreserved commitment might involve,
we tell ourselves that you will understand if we
make compromises
and tone down the message of the gospel;

that you will make allowances for our mistakes,
so we needn't try too hard to live up to your example.
Forgive us for abusing your grace and evading
your challenge,
for effectively denying your transforming power
through the narrowness of our vision
and the weakness of our faith.
Teach us to focus on your grace and goodness,
so that, though we will never be quite like you,
we may at least have the chance of getting closer.
In your name we ask it. *Nick Fawcett*

66 Lord Jesus Christ,
thank you for staying true to your calling to the very end,
refusing to compromise your mission in any way.
Thank you for all those who have followed in your footsteps,
giving their all for the sake of the gospel.
Teach us to walk faithfully in your way
rather than follow the course of least resistance,
to stand up for what we believe
rather than go along with the crowd.
Help us to understand all you have done for us,
and so may our lives be spent in your service,
to the glory of your name. *Nick Fawcett*

67 Lord Jesus Christ,
we bear your name and we profess to follow your way,
yet there is little if anything different about us from
anyone else.
We have failed you in so many ways;
our faith weak,
our love poor
and our commitment unpredictable.
We have been half-hearted in your service,
concerned more about our own interests than your glory.
All too often our words say one thing but our deeds another,
the message we proclaim belied by the way we live,
so that instead of leading people towards you we lead
them away.

Forgive us and help us to follow you not just in name only
but also in truth,
proud to be identified with your cause
and committing our lives to the work of your kingdom.
We ask it for your name's sake.   *Nick Fawcett*

68   Lord Jesus Christ,
     we talk about belonging to you and offering you our service,
     but so often reality falls short of the ideal.
     Instead of making you an integral part of our lives,
     we treat you as an optional extra,
     there to turn to as and when it suits us.
     Instead of working for your kingdom,
     we strive solely to serve our own interests.
     Instead of involving ourselves in the life of your people,
     we stay on the fringes,
     reluctant to commit ourselves wholly to your cause.
     Our deeds deny our words;
     our lives betray our lack of faith.
     Forgive us and save us from confusing nominal Christianity
     with living discipleship.
     Teach us what it means to belong to you
     and to be part of your Church,
     and so may we serve you as you deserve,
     to the glory of your name.   *Nick Fawcett*

69   Lord Jesus Christ,
     we want to commit ourselves to your service
     and we do our best to follow you,
     but we are led astray so easily,
     our faith so weak and temptation so strong.
     We think we have turned our back on our old ways,
     only to find them resurfacing in another guise.
     We try to let go of self,
     only to discover it still holds us firmly in its grip.
     For all our good intentions,
     we find ourselves caught between two worlds,
     unable to escape the hold of one
     yet incapable of fully embracing the other.

Forgive us the many times we fail you,
and give us strength,
when our allegiance is tested,
to put you first.
Help us not simply to call you Lord,
but to make you the Lord of our lives,
to the glory of your name.   *Nick Fawcett*

70 Lord Jesus Christ,
when we think of your commitment to us
and your willingness to face suffering and death on our behalf,
we are ashamed of our disloyalty to you
and our failure to stand up for your kingdom.
We keep quiet about our faith for fear of embarrassment.
We close our eyes and ears to wrongdoing,
rather than risk unpopularity.
We water down our principles for the sake of an easy peace.
We avoid getting involved in needs around us,
claiming they are none of our business.
In so many ways, we let you down,
offering you an empty, secret discipleship.
Forgive us our weakness and cowardice,
and give us courage to stand up for what we believe in
and proudly to declare you as Lord of our lives,
to the glory of your name.   *Nick Fawcett*

71 Lord Jesus Christ,
you tell us to walk in the light,
and to witness to it through the things we do and the
people we are.
You call us to let your light shine through us
so that others might see and give glory to God.
Forgive us that all too often we do the opposite,
hiding our light under a bushel,
even sometimes to the point of secret discipleship.
Afraid of what others might think
and concerned that admitting faith in you
might prejudice our standing in this world,
we keep our beliefs private.

Forgive us the feebleness of our commitment
and the weakness of our love.
Help us to recognise everything you have done for us,
and so teach us to acknowledge you proudly as the light of
our lives,
whatever the cost might be.
In your name we pray.   *Nick Fawcett*

72   Loving God,
     you ask us whatever we do,
     to do it for your sake –
     to offer our whole life,
     our every thought,
     word and action –
     to your service and for your glory.
     Help us to understand what that really means –
     to see every part of each day as an opportunity to work
     for you.
     Teach us to do everything in such a way
     that your hand may be evident upon us,
     your Spirit unmistakably at work
     and your love clear to all,
     to the glory of your name.   *Nick Fawcett*

73   Gracious God,
     show us where our discipleship is weak,
     our commitment flawed and our lives found wanting
     and, by your grace,
     help us to become more like the people you would have
     us be,
     through Jesus Christ our Lord.   *Nick Fawcett*

74   Living God,
     send us back to our journey of discipleship redeemed in love,
     renewed in faith,
     restored in strength and refreshed in spirit,
     in the name of the risen Christ who goes before us.
                                                         Nick Fawcett

75 Lord Jesus Christ,
    teach us what it means to be a disciple,
    and, by your grace,
    help us to respond and to be followers of your way,
    to the glory of your name.   *Nick Fawcett*

76 The Lord watch over us,
    his hands below,
    his arms around and his Spirit within,
    and so may he lead us this and every day
    as we travel along life's chequered path.
    In the name of Christ.   *Nick Fawcett*

77 May the word of God guide our footsteps,
    the power of God equip us for service,
    the grace of God renew us
    and the love of God surround us always.
    May Christ be our constant companion on the path
    of discipleship,
    until our journey is over and we meet with God face to face,
    secure in the joy of his everlasting kingdom.
    In his name we ask it.   *Nick Fawcett*

78 Living God,
    embrace us in your arms,
    encircle us with your grace,
    enfold us in your love,
    and lead us safely onward until our journey is over
    and you are all in all.   *Nick Fawcett*

79 Living God,
    help us to meet difficulties and disappointments
    with confidence,
    knowing that you will equip us to respond
    to whatever may be asked of us.   *Nick Fawcett*

80 Lord Jesus Christ,
    inspire us through your love
    and the great company of those who have gone before us,
    to persevere and run the race,
    to the glory of your name.   *Nick Fawcett*

81 Living God,
    when what you ask seems beyond us,
    help us to trust in your purpose,
    and if we meet with failure,
    teach us not to lose faith but to try and keep on trying,
    in Christ's name.   *Nick Fawcett*

82 Living God,
    open our eyes to the great adventure of faith
    and to the unfathomable mysteries of your purpose,
    and so help us to live as pilgrims,
    travelling together in hope.   *Nick Fawcett*

83 Lord Jesus Christ,
    help us to walk the journey to which you have called us,
    keeping faith in your saving purpose.
    When we grow weary, revive us;
    when we go astray, direct us;
    when we lose heart, inspire us,
    and when we turn back reprove us.
    Keep us travelling ever onwards,
    trusting in your guidance
    and certain that you will be there at our journey's end,
    to welcome us home into your eternal kingdom.
    In your name we ask it.   *Nick Fawcett*

84 Living God,
    hold on to us, keep us steady,
    and direct our footsteps; and, if we stumble,
    lead us on to the way of life once more
    so that we may continue safely until our journey's end.
    In the name of Christ we ask it.   *Nick Fawcett*

85 Lord Jesus Christ,
though the journey is long
and we encounter obstacles along the way,
help us to keep on searching to know you better,
until that day when we enter your kingdom
and meet you face to face.   *Nick Fawcett*

86 Sovereign God,
rekindle our vision,
revive our faith
and renew our resolve to take up our cross.
Show us the way in Christ and give us faith to follow,
for his name's sake.   *Nick Fawcett*

87 Sovereign God,
when we are led astray,
call us back and help us to walk your way more faithfully,
to our journey's end.   *Nick Fawcett*

88 Sovereign God,
renew our faith, revive our hope,
restore our trust, rekindle our vision,
and so may we serve you in quiet confidence,
this day and always.   *Nick Fawcett*

89 Lord Jesus Christ,
teach us to travel light
and to let go of all that may encumber us on our journey.
So may we walk your way faithfully to the end,
to the glory of your name.   *Nick Fawcett*

90 Living God,
we thank you that,
wherever we are, whatever we face,
you are with us, through Christ,
constantly by our side,
travelling with us and looking to lead us forward
into new experiences of your love.
Receive our praise,
through Jesus Christ our Lord.   *Nick Fawcett*

91   Sovereign God,
open our hearts to all you have yet to say,
do and teach.
Help us, whoever we may be,
to recognise that, however far we have come,
our journey has only just begun,
and so may we continue to explore the wonder of your love
and the mystery of your gracious purpose,
this day and for evermore.   *Nick Fawcett*

92   Loving God,
teach us to walk with you,
confident that, though we do not know the way,
you will guide our footsteps to our journey's end.
                                              Nick Fawcett

93   Lord Jesus Christ,
you call us to walk in faith,
but we so rarely do that.
We follow for a time,
but we are quickly led astray.
When your message is too demanding,
when you ask from us what we would rather not give,
and when your words make us feel uncomfortable,
striking too near the mark,
then we turn away from you,
resisting your call.
When other interests conflict with discipleship,
when the demands and responsibilities of each day crowd in
upon us,
we are swift to forget you,
ignoring your will in preference to our own.
When life is hard and things do not go as we had hoped,
faith gives way to doubt and we lose sight of your promises.
Forgive that shallowness of our commitment,
and grant light to our path,
so that we may step forward in faith
and travel onwards wherever you might lead,
through Jesus Christ our Lord.   *Nick Fawcett*

94 Gracious God,
we thank you for the great adventure of life
in all its endless diversity and richness.
We thank you that there is always more to learn,
more to explore
and more to experience.
Keep our minds open to that special truth
for, as the years pass,
we sometimes lose our sense of childlike wonder and
fascination,
becoming worldly-wise or blasé about life,
taking for granted those things that once stirred
our imagination,
and so sinking into an ever-deeper rut of cynicism and
over-familiarity.
Help us to recapture something of the innocence
and spontaneity
of our childhood years:
the ability to look at the world with inquiring eyes,
to trust in the future
and to celebrate the present.
Gracious God,
give us faith in life
and faith in you,
through Jesus Christ our Lord. *Nick Fawcett*

95 Living God,
we have committed ourselves to the path of discipleship
and we want to walk it faithfully,
but we know how easy it is to slip back.
Help us to be alert to dangers,
able to recognise those things that might trip us up.
Help us to keep our eyes on you,
knowing that you will lead us safely
through the pitfalls and obstacles in our path.
And, should we stumble or find ourselves slipping,
hold on to us,
keep us steady
and direct our footsteps

so that we will find the path once more
and continue safely on our way
until our journey's end.
In Christ's name we ask it.   *Nick Fawcett*

96   Lord God,
you know that life isn't always easy.
There are times when we feel exhausted,
overwhelmed, defeated.
Remind us then of those who have gone before us,
keeping the faith
and running the race with perseverance.
Remind us of the fellowship we share with all your people,
and the strength we can gain from one another.
Remind us of our responsibility to those who will come
after us,
the example we need to set to encourage and inspire them.
Above all, remind us of Jesus,
his willingness to endure the cross for our sake,
his faithfulness to the end.
So give us strength to battle on,
faithful in turn,
in the knowledge that you are waiting to receive us
and to grant us the joy of your kingdom,
the prize of everlasting life,
through Jesus Christ our Lord.   *Nick Fawcett*

97   Living God,
we do not find it easy to journey in faith.
We want a clearer idea of what the future holds,
a knowledge of where we are heading
and an explanation of how we are going to get there.
Yet neither life nor faith is like that,
few things as definite as we would like them to be.
Inspire us, though, by the knowledge that you are
journeying with us
every step of the way.
May that truth equip us with courage to step out into
the unknown,

with faith to follow wherever you lead,
with trust to walk with humility
and with commitment to travel on to our journey's end,
through Jesus Christ our Lord.   *Nick Fawcett*

98   Lord Jesus Christ,
it is not easy to follow you;
not if we are serious about discipleship.
You challenge our whole perspective on life,
calling us not just to a statement of belief but to a way of life.
You are always leading us forward,
eager to guide us into new experiences of your love
and a deeper understanding of your purpose,
yet so often we refuse to follow where you would have us go.
Forgive us for losing the sense of direction
that marked our early days of discipleship.
Forgive us for trusting you when all goes well
but doubting the moment life fails to conform to
our expectations.
Forgive us for thinking that we have done all that needs to
be done,
imagining that one simple confession of faith suffices for
a lifetime.
Lord,
you are still calling,
inviting us to respond.
Help us to follow.   *Nick Fawcett*

99   Living God,
speak to us through everything life has brought us today,
good and bad, pleasure or pain,
and so help us to be better equipped
to serve and love you in the days ahead,
to the glory of your name.   *Nick Fawcett*

100   Eternal God,
though darkness falls and night comes upon us,
keep us always in the light of your love
and the radiance of your presence,
through Jesus Christ our Lord.   *Nick Fawcett*

101   Mighty God,
for all the ways you have been with us this day,
protecting, providing,
instructing, inspiring,
we give you our praise,
in the name of Christ.   *Nick Fawcett*

102   Gracious God,
for all that this day has brought us
we offer you our thanks.
Recognised or unrecognised,
seen or unseen,
you have been there,
taking our hand to lead us forward.
In the knowledge of all you have done and will yet do,
we will take our rest,
in peace and quiet confidence.   *Nick Fawcett*

103   Lord Jesus Christ,
the same yesterday, today and tomorrow,
we thank you for all we have experienced today,
we trust you for all we shall experience tomorrow.
Always you are faithful,
worthy of honour and adulation.
Receive, then, our joyful worship,
in the name of Christ.   *Nick Fawcett*

104   Lord Jesus Christ,
enfold us in your peace,
encircle us with your love,
and so may we pass this night
and live our days in quietness of mind and tranquillity
of spirit,
through Jesus Christ our Lord.   *Nick Fawcett*

105   Loving God,
thank you for all we have done this day
and forgive us for all we should have done but failed to do.
                                          Nick Fawcett

106 Living God,
  remind us that worship without action,
  faith without deeds,
  is like a well without water,
  a book without words –
  promising much yet yielding nothing.
  Teach us, then, to practise our faith
  rather than simply profess it,
  for your name's sake.   *Nick Fawcett*

107 Lord Jesus Christ,
  you know that we want to follow you,
  but you know also how hard we find it to do so.
  Despite our good intentions,
  we repeatedly slip back into our old ways,
  pursuing our own ends rather than your will.
  Instead of working and witnessing for you,
  we are lukewarm in service and weak in discipleship.
  Instead of growing,
  our faith has become stale and tired,
  no longer challenging or inspiring us
  as in the days when we first believed.
  Forgive us for falling away so easily.
  Cleanse, renew and restore us by your redeeming touch,
  and help us to live for you today, tomorrow and every day,
  sure and steadfast,
  to the glory of your name.   *Nick Fawcett*

108 Loving God,
  occasionally there are moments that we never want to end,
  moments so special that we wish time would stand still
  so that we could hold on to them for ever,
  but we know that life and faith are not like that,
  instead always needing to move on if they are not to
  grow stale.
  Help us, then, to be open to new experiences of your love,
  new insights into your greatness,
  new responses to your call,
  and a new awareness of your guidance,

so that we may know you better each day,
until that time we rejoice in your presence for all eternity,
in the joy of Christ that will never fade or perish.
In his name we ask it.   *Nick Fawcett*

109 Lord Jesus Christ,
we remember your words to the disciples
that the kingdom of heaven belongs to little children,
and we remember also your warning that unless we
become like children,
we can never hope to enter that kingdom.
Teach us what that means.
Grant us the childlike qualities we need to grow in faith –
a child's innocence and hunger to learn,
a child's love and total trust.
Help us,
like them,
to step out gladly into the great adventure of faith,
to the glory of your name.   *Nick Fawcett*

110 Almighty God,
teach us to remember all you have done
and to give you the praise you deserve.
Teach us each day to recall your creative acts,
your mighty deeds throughout history,
and your faithful dealings with your people across the years.
Above all, teach us to remember your graciousness in
Jesus Christ –
your coming, living, dying and rising among us,
so that we might have life in all its fullness.
For the memory of such things,
and the constant reminder of them we receive each day,
we give you our thanks and praise,
through Jesus Christ our Lord.   *Nick Fawcett*

111 Almighty God,
we remember again all you have done across the years:
your creative acts,
your mighty deeds throughout history,
your gift of Jesus Christ.

We remember all you have done for us:
your sovereign love,
your gracious mercy and your constant guidance every day
of our lives.
Forgive us that so often and so easily we forget those things,
brooding instead over our troubles,
coveting what we do not have,
preoccupied with our personal well-being rather than
your kingdom.
Help us each day to remind ourselves of your goodness,
to recall the ways you have blessed us,
and so to keep you at the forefront of our lives,
living and working for your glory.
In Christ's name we ask it.   *Nick Fawcett*

112   God of truth, justice and power,
      we praise you that you are also a God of love.
      Though we disobey your commandments
      and lose sight of your goodness,
      though we fail to love others and are forgetful of you,
      still you love us.
      Though we reject your guidance,
      betray our convictions and deny our calling,
      still you care.
      Always you are there,
      watching over us,
      calling us back,
      welcoming us home.
      Day after day we receive new blessings, mercy and strength
      from your loving hands.
      Gracious God,
      we praise you for your awesome love and your great
      faithfulness,
      in the name of Christ.   *Nick Fawcett*

113   Gracious God,
      we thank you that you are here by our side,
      wanting to meet us,
      greet us
      and teach us.

We thank you for being with us everywhere –
at every moment,
every place and every occasion –
watching over us as a father watches over his child.
Day by day,
you stay close –
recognised or unrecognised,
remembered or forgotten,
obeyed or disobeyed,
acknowledged or taken for granted.
Though our response to you is varied and our commitment
wavering,
you are always the same:
ever-faithful,
all-loving,
always true.
We have no way of knowing what the future may hold,
whether for good or ill,
but what we do know,
and hold on to,
is that you will remain the same,
always there when we need you,
and that nothing finally can ever separate us
from your love in Christ.
For that assurance,
receive our praise,
in his name.

Nick Fawcett

114   Living God,
help us to remember that you are a God who never sleeps,
a God on whom we can depend in any and every situation.
When we feel lost and alone,
teach us that you are there.
When we feel overwhelmed by trouble,
unsure of our ability to get through,
help us to remember that you are close by.
When we feel uncertain of the way ahead,
fearful of what the future may hold,
teach us that you are watching over us.

Help us to understand that, whatever we may face,
you will guide and guard us,
protecting us from evil
and enfolding us in your everlasting arms,
and in that knowledge may we meet every day with
quiet trust
and glad thanksgiving,
in Christ's name.   *Nick Fawcett*

115   Lord Jesus Christ,
thank you for the way you watch over us throughout
our lives,
the way you are continually there to guard and guide us,
whatever we may face.
When we wander far from your side,
you do not abandon us to our fate but instead come
looking for us,
your love refusing to let us go.
Though we may forsake you,
you never forsake us.
Though we are faithless,
you remain faithful.
We praise you for that great truth,
and we ask forgiveness for the areas in our lives
in which we continue to go astray.
Help us to follow you more closely in the days ahead,
to the glory of your name.   *Nick Fawcett*

116   Loving God,
thank you for this day and all the opportunities it brings:
moments to work and rest,
to give and receive,
to wonder and worship.
Thank you for having been with us throughout our lives –
always there to guide our footsteps and lead us forward.
Thank you for the assurance of your continuing guidance –
the knowledge that whatever the future may bring,
whatever challenges we may face or trials we may endure,
you will be there to see us through,

giving us the strength and resources we need,
and a joy that cannot be shaken.
God of past, present and future,
the same yesterday, today and tomorrow,
we praise you for each and every moment,
and consecrate them all to your service.
We ask it in the name of Christ.   *Nick Fawcett*

117 Loving God,
we know we shouldn't be afraid but sometimes we are –
afraid of what the future might hold
and whether we will have the strength to meet it.
Thank you for the assurance that whatever we may face,
you will be there beside us.
Thank you for your promise to lift us up and help us to
start again,
however often we may fail.
Thank you for the times you have reached out in the past,
the experiences we can look back on
when your arms have been there to support us
when we needed them most.
Teach us to trust you more completely
and so to step out in faith,
confident that, though we may stumble,
you will set us on our feet once more.   *Nick Fawcett*

118 Loving God,
we thank you for all the ways you are with us
and all the ways you grant your blessing.
We thank you for the guidance you give,
the strength you supply,
the mercy you show
and the love with which you surround us.
We thank you that your purpose extends beyond this life
into eternity;
that you are holding the best in store.
Teach us to walk with you each day
knowing you are always by our side,
and so may we trust you for the future,
secure in the everlasting hope you have given us in Christ,
that nothing shall ever destroy.   *Nick Fawcett*

119 Loving God,
we thank you that you are a God we can depend on,
a God in whom we can put our trust.
What you promise is done;
what you purpose is fulfilled.
We remember your promise to Abraham –
that, through his offspring, all the world would be blessed;
to Moses –
that you would lead the Israelites out of Egypt;
to Isaiah –
that you would deliver your people from exile;
to your prophets –
that the Messiah would come;
to the Apostles –
that he would rise again on the third day.
We thank you that you fulfilled those promises,
just as you said you would –
your Son born from the line of Abraham,
your chosen nation set free from slavery,
your people returning joyfully to Jerusalem,
your promised deliverer born in Bethlehem,
your power seen in the resurrection of Christ.
We thank you for what that means for us today –
that we can live each moment with confidence,
whatever our circumstances may be,
whatever times of testing may befall us,
knowing that, though all else may fail,
you will not;
though heaven and earth may pass away,
your words will endure for ever.
So we look forward to that day when your purpose is
fulfilled
and you are all in all.
Until then, we will trust in you,
secure in your love,
confident in your eternal purpose,
assured that your will shall be done.
Receive our thanks,
in the name of Christ.

Nick Fawcett

120   Faithful God,
teach us to be content with what we have
rather than to bemoan what we wish we had;
to focus on what we need
rather than dwell on what we want;
to appreciate the essentials of life
rather than constantly to crave its luxuries.
Help us, in other words,
to celebrate the things that matter,
and to let go of those that don't.
In Christ's name we pray.   *Nick Fawcett*

121   Lord Jesus Christ,
we know that true riches do not lie on earth
and yet we find it hard truly to accept that fact.
Day after day,
we strive to put a bit of extra money into our pocket,
and we yearn to splash out a little,
to treat ourselves to those few extra luxuries,
to afford our dream holiday, new car or luxury home.
We find it hard to see beyond the alluring pleasures of this
material world,
even though we know that so much of what it seems to
offer is illusory,
unable to satisfy for more than a few moments,
let alone to meet our deepest needs.
Open our eyes to true riches:
to the blessings you have given us
and to all that you yet hold in store.
Help us to appreciate the joy and fulfilment that you alone
can offer,
and to celebrate the inheritance beyond price
that comes through knowing and serving you.
We ask it in your name.   *Nick Fawcett*

122   Eternal God,
we spend so much of our lives seeking happiness,
yet much of the time we are frustrated.

We turn from one thing to another,
believing for a moment that it may offer the fulfilment
we crave,
but so many pleasures are fleeting,
here today and gone tomorrow.
There are times when life seems empty,
when nothing seems permanent,
not even those things most precious to us.
Help us to find the rest for our souls that you alone can give;
to discover in you that inner peace which can never change
but which will go on satisfying for all eternity.
Help us to live each day in tune with you,
rejoicing in all you have given
and anticipating all you have yet to give,
through Christ our Lord.   *Nick Fawcett*

123   Gracious God,
we know we can never repay the love you have shown us,
but we long to show our gratitude by loving you in return,
by serving you as you desire,
by being the sort of people you call us to be.
Set us free from our preoccupation with the things of
this world,
from our obsession with self,
from the pride, greed and envy
which blind us to all that really matters.
Teach us to live according to the values of your kingdom,
where it is in giving that we shall receive,
in letting go that we shall find,
in being poor that we shall become rich.
Take us and use us, by your grace,
through Jesus Christ our Lord.   *Nick Fawcett*

124   Loving God,
thank you for your great gift of life in all its fullness –
everything you have given to enjoy,
celebrate and live for.
Thank you for the innumerable blessings you shower upon
us every day:

love to share,
beauty to enthral,
health to enjoy,
food to eat and so much more –
a world to excite, fascinate and savour.
Above all, thank you for the life you have given us in Christ;
a life that you want us and all people to enjoy
not just now but for all eternity.
Teach us to celebrate your love in all its richness,
to rejoice in your gifts in all their abundance
and to celebrate life in all its fullness,
to the glory of your name.   *Nick Fawcett*

125 Living God,
we have so much to celebrate,
more than previous generations would have
imagined possible,
yet it does not bring us peace.
We still worry about the future and brood over the past;
still fret over money, work or loved ones,
and still wrestle with pressures, fears, anxieties and questions.
For all their sophistication and ingenuity,
the technology and wealth of modern society cannot meet
our deepest needs,
nor calm the storm within.
So we come to you who alone can nourish our souls
and renew our being –
the one in whom we find not the extras of life but life itself.
Teach us to measure all else against who and what you are,
and, in getting that into perspective,
may we discover the peace you promise to all who know you,
through Jesus Christ our Lord.   *Nick Fawcett*

126 Gracious God,
we do not come today under any illusions,
with any sense that we are righteous,
deserving
or better than others.

We come because we know we are none of these –
because our faults are all too clear to us,
our weaknesses starkly apparent.
We come, then, throwing ourselves upon your mercy,
begging for forgiveness,
a fresh start,
a new heart and right spirit within us.
Renew us, we pray,
for we cannot do it ourselves.
Receive, accept and use us by your grace,
for your kingdom.   *Nick Fawcett*

127   Gracious God,
though we have repeatedly forgotten you –
going our own way,
squandering your blessing
and ignoring your will –
teach us that you long still to welcome us back,
your arms constantly outstretched to embrace us once more.
In that faith we come now,
praising you for your goodness,
acknowledging our many faults,
thanking you for your mercy
and seeking to love and serve you better.
Receive us
and help us to open our hearts as wide to you
as yours is open to us.   *Nick Fawcett*

128   Gracious God,
we dare to draw near,
not through any merit of our own
but trusting in your great mercy –
redeemed, renewed and restored through the love of Christ.
Set us free from all that holds us captive;
we gladly surrender our lives to your service,
to be used as you will.
As you have given,
so we give back,
in the name of Christ.   *Nick Fawcett*

129   Sovereign God,
we come to you conscious of all that is wrong in our lives,
aware that we have no claim on your goodness
nor any merit that might lead us to expect it.
Yet we come knowing that you are a God of love,
slow to anger and swift to show mercy;
a God who yearns to put the past behind us
and to help us start again,
if only we are truly sorry and sincerely wish it.
So, then, we dare to approach,
trusting in your gracious love, so wonderfully revealed
in Christ,
and, in penitence, seeking forgiveness and new beginnings.
Through your Son, put your hand upon us,
lift us up,
restore us
and send us on our way to live and work for you,
in his name.
                                                                Nick Fawcett

130   Lord Jesus Christ,
reach out to us through this time of worship,
and touch our lives
with your cleansing, healing, restoring and renewing power.
Speak to us your word of forgiveness and peace,
and, through your Spirit, move within us,
encouraging,
enthusing,
equipping,
enabling.
Encircle us in your love
and enfold us in your grace,
that we might find inner wholeness in body, mind and spirit,
this and every day.
                                           Nick Fawcett

131   Lord,
open our mouths that we might declare your praise;
open our ears that we might hear your voice;
open our hearts that our lives might be open in turn
to you and others.

Teach us that your grace,
your word and your love
are for us and everyone,
without partiality,
your concern reaching to the ends of the earth –
to people of every race, faith, culture and status –
no one in your eyes of more or less worth than others.
Teach us, then, through our worship,
how much you value us and everyone.   *Nick Fawcett*

132   Gracious God,
      we praise you that you welcome us into your presence
      despite all that is unworthy in our lives:
      all our faults, failings, falsehoods and faithlessness.
      Speak to us through your willingness to forgive and go
      on forgiving,
      and so help us to forgive in turn,
      striving to heal broken relationships,
      mend quarrels,
      let bygones be bygones
      and start afresh.
      Teach us through the example of Christ
      to show something of the mercy you have shown to us.
      In his name we pray.   *Nick Fawcett*

133   Loving God,
      conscious of our repeated disobedience to your will
      and our inability to serve you as we would like,
      we find it hard sometimes to believe you still have time
      for us,
      still delight in our presence and value our worship.
      Yet you teach us that your nature is to forgive
      and go on forgiving.
      Remind us of that now,
      and help us to come truly penitent
      but also truly confident that your love continues
      and your mercy endures.
      Nurture, then, the faith you have sown within us,
      and, by your grace, help it to grow,
      so that our lives may fully bear fruit in your service.
                                                 Nick Fawcett

134 Lord Jesus Christ,
we know that, whatever we give you,
it can never begin to repay the price you paid to redeem us,
nor ever earn the love you so freely showed,
but we want to tell you how grateful we are
for your awesome love and immense sacrifice.
We want to proffer a token of our love
and a sign of our commitment;
to respond to the joy you've brought us
through offering heartfelt praise and committed service,
honouring to you and pleasing in your sight.
Receive, then, the worship we bring,
the faith we declare
and the discipleship we offer,
for, poor though they may be,
we offer them with body, mind and soul
humbly to you. *Nick Fawcett*

135 Eternal God,
put your hand upon us,
your arms around us,
and your Spirit within us,
so that we may recognise your presence,
hear your voice,
receive your guidance
and grasp more of who and what you are,
through Jesus Christ our Lord. *Nick Fawcett*

136 Prince of Peace, heal us.
Lamb of God, redeem us.
Shepherd of the sheep, guard us.
Light of the world, lead us.
Lord Jesus Christ, touch our lives by your grace,
and help us to live and work for you, to your glory.
Nick Fawcett

137 Sovereign God,
open our hearts afresh to the wonder of your presence,
the awesomeness of your power,
the breadth of your love and the extent of your purpose.
So may we live each day to the glory of your name.
Nick Fawcett

138 Lord Jesus Christ,
  draw close to us and help us to draw closer to you,
  so that we may know and love you better
  and follow more faithfully as your disciples,
  now and always.   *Nick Fawcett*

139 Living God,
  when we forget you, fail you
  and wander far from your side,
  draw near by your grace,
  and open our hearts afresh to your love,
  through Jesus Christ our Lord.   *Nick Fawcett*

140 Lord Jesus Christ,
  help us to turn from everything that leads us astray,
  and to focus on you and your will,
  for your name's sake.   *Nick Fawcett*

141 Sovereign God,
  give us today a deeper sense of who and what you are,
  and may we acknowledge your greatness through word
  and deed,
  to the glory of your name.   *Nick Fawcett*

142 Gracious God,
  nurture the seed of faith within us.
  Help us to grow closer to you and to Christ,
  and so cultivate within us the fruits you hunger to see,
  through the grace of Jesus Christ, our Lord.   *Nick Fawcett*

143 Loving God,
  take what we are and remould us by your grace,
  so that we will bear the image of Christ within us,
  and live to his glory.   *Nick Fawcett*

144 Living God,
  we know what our lives ought to be like,
  we know what they are,
  and we are ashamed at the difference between the two.

Where we ought to reveal Christ,
we show only ourselves.
Where we ought to bear witness to his life-changing power,
we demonstrate instead how little has actually changed.
So much about us denies rather than affirms the gospel,
leading people to dismiss its claims
rather than to explore them further.
Forgive us for all that is wrong
and, by your Spirit, clothe us with joy,
peace,
patience,
kindness,
generosity,
faithfulness,
gentleness,
self-control,
and, above all, love.
Work in our lives,
and so work through us to speak to others,
through the grace of Christ.   *Nick Fawcett*

145 Living God,
we talk of commitment,
yet so often we are casual about our faith
and complacent in discipleship.
We neglect your word
and fail to make time for prayer or quiet reflection,
thus giving ourselves little opportunity to hear you.
Instead of seeking to grow in faith,
we assume we have advanced as far as we need to.
Forgive us our feeble vision and lack of dedication.
Instil in us a new sense of purpose and a greater resolve to
fulfil our goals,
and so help us to achieve the prize
to which you have called us in Jesus Christ,
for his name's sake.   *Nick Fawcett*

146 Lord Jesus Christ,
   there is so much within us that is not as it should be:
   thoughts, attitudes, desires and fears
   that alienate us from others and from you
   and that disturb, divide and ultimately destroy.
   We long to be like you:
   to feel the same love and compassion that you felt,
   to experience the same closeness with God,
   and to know the same inner wholeness and harmony.
   Alone, though, we cannot achieve it,
   no amount of effort sufficient to help us emulate
   your example.
   Draw closer to us through your grace,
   and fill us in body, mind and soul.
   Speak to us,
   teach and guide,
   so that we may know you better.
   Work within our hearts,
   transforming the clay of our lives into a new creation,
   moulded by your hands.
   In your name we ask it.   *Nick Fawcett*

147 Lord Jesus Christ,
   we thank you that discipleship is not finally about what we
   can do for you
   but about what you have done for us.
   We praise you that your love does not depend on our works
   but on your grace.
   We celebrate with wonder your presence within us;
   the way you have come into our lives
   to offer your guidance, strength, peace and joy.
   Fill us a little more each day,
   so that we may know you better and become more like you,
   our lives testifying to your sovereign and renewing power.
                                                       Nick Fawcett

148 Lord,
   there is so much in the gospel that goes against the grain:
   your call to deny ourselves and put others first;
   your command to love our enemies and turn the other cheek;

your challenge to forgive and go on forgiving.
All this,
and so much else,
runs contrary to our natural inclinations,
contradicting the received wisdom of this world.
We do not find it easy and at times we resist,
yet we know that in you and you alone is the path to life –
the way to peace, joy and fulfilment.
Take us, then, and fashion our lives according to your pattern,
until your will becomes our will
and your way our way.
In the name of Christ we ask it.   *Nick Fawcett*

149 Living God,
we thank you for the seed of faith you have sown within us
and for the way it has grown across the years,
but we confess also that there are times when all is not as it
should be.
Instead of continuing to flourish,
our commitment starts to flag and our vision to wilt,
cramped by the narrowness of our horizons,
suffocated by complacency and starved of space in which
to expand.
Forgive us for allowing that to happen and accepting it as
the norm.
Help us to open our lives to you
so that you can feed us through your word,
nourish us through your Spirit
and nurture us through the gracious love of Christ,
in whose name we pray.   *Nick Fawcett*

150 Living God,
we turned to you once
and, naively, we imagined we had done all that needed doing;
that from then on we would say goodbye to our old self
and live in newness of life.
The reality, we have found, is that two selves war within us.
Help us, then, to turn to you once more,
and to go on doing so for however long it takes.

Help us, each day, to put off the old self
and to be renewed in body, mind and spirit through
your grace,
until in the fullness of time you have finished your
redemptive work
and made of us a new creation,
through Jesus Christ our Lord.   *Nick Fawcett*

151   Loving God,
       help us, as we worship you, to look honestly at ourselves
       and recognise where we fail you,
       where our lives fall short,
       where our commitment is weak,
       where the harvest is poor.
       Come to us afresh,
       and bring growth in grace,
       fresh shoots of the Spirit,
       signs of new life.
       In your mercy, nurture our faith,
       so that we might bear fruit for you,
       reflecting your love
       and living to your praise and glory,
       through Jesus Christ our Lord.   *Nick Fawcett*

152   God of all,
       we thirst to know you better,
       to grow closer to you each day.
       Reach out now and speak your word of life.
       Equip us to worship you in Spirit and in truth,
       so that your grace may pour upon us,
       and your love well up in our hearts,
       refreshing, reviving and renewing,
       satisfying body, mind and soul.
       Meet us here, in all our weakness,
       and grant us the living water that you alone can give,
       through Jesus Christ our Lord.   *Nick Fawcett*

153   Gracious God,
       open our hearts afresh today
       to the fullness of life you want us to experience,

not only in eternity but also here and now –
life lived in union with you,
in harmony with your will
and in the light of your love.
Draw us closer to your side,
so that whatever separates us from you,
undermining the unity you want us to enjoy,
will be overcome,
our lives in consequence bearing witness to you,
so that others in turn
might know and believe in you for themselves,
through Jesus Christ our Lord.   *Nick Fawcett*

154   Spirit of God,
fill us now as we worship you.
Sanctify our listening and thinking,
our giving and doing,
so that all we offer and all we are
may reach up to you and out to others,
in impulsive praise and joyful service.
Teach, equip, guide and inspire us
this and every day.   *Nick Fawcett*

155   Gracious God,
remind us as we worship you
that you see not the outside but the person beneath;
that you look beyond appearances to the thoughts of
the heart.
Save us, then, from empty show or superficial piety,
and teach us to approach you instead in faith and humility,
knowing that your love extends to all who truly seek you,
through Jesus Christ our Lord.   *Nick Fawcett*

156   Lord Jesus Christ,
as you taught the crowds on the mountaintop,
so now teach us as we gather in your name.
Prompt us through your Spirit,
that we might hear and understand your word.

Help us to listen and learn,
reflecting on what you say to us and applying it to our lives,
so that our words and deeds might bear witness to you,
your light shining through us,
to the glory of God the Father. *Nick Fawcett*

157   Send us out, Lord, with hearts full of expectation,
confident that the future is in your hands –
that, as you have blessed us,
so you will bless us again,
each day bringing new beginnings. *Nick Fawcett*

158   Loving God,
we cannot see you except through Christ;
we cannot come to Christ unless you draw us to him;
and so we approach you again,
recognising our need,
our dependence on you,
and asking you to create and increase our faith,
helping us to believe not just nominally
but with body, mind and soul,
with our whole heart and being.
Hear us
and answer our prayer,
through Jesus Christ our Lord. *Nick Fawcett*

159   Lord Jesus Christ,
save us from losing sight of why we are here;
from speaking and failing to listen,
from giving and forgetting to receive,
from praying and refusing to hear,
from looking but failing to seek.
Open our lips to praise you,
our eyes to see you,
our ears to hear you and our lives to serve you,
to the glory of your name. *Nick Fawcett*

160 Sovereign God,
come among us, upon us
and within us through your Holy Spirit,
so that we may be equipped both to know your will
and to do it.
Grant us an inner experience of your presence,
so that your word might be unfolded,
your peace given,
your love nurtured
and your power imparted,
such that we may honour you not just here and now
but in every place and at all times,
through keeping your commands and observing your will.
In Christ's name we pray.   *Nick Fawcett*

161 Almighty God,
help us to grasp more clearly today that,
for all your purity, holiness, righteousness and power,
you call us your children,
wanting us to relate to you as our Father –
one who values every one of us,
who takes pleasure in our presence
and who delights to give us good things.
Teach us to live in the light of that truth,
turning to you each day
for the guidance and blessing you so long to provide,
seeking above all the indwelling of your Spirit,
through which you live in us and we can live in you.
In Christ's name we pray.   *Nick Fawcett*

162 Gracious God,
for the assurance that in you we will find the meaning
we seek,
the end of all our striving, receive our praise.
May that truth inspire and instruct our continuing search
for understanding
until that day we see and know you face to face and all
is answered,
through Jesus Christ our Lord.   *Nick Fawcett*

163 Living God,
before we ask for anything, teach us what to ask for;
before we seek your blessing, teach us what that means;
before we presume to knock, teach us which door to choose.
Guide us in your ways,
through Jesus Christ our Lord.   *Nick Fawcett*

164 Living God,
time and again we ask you to speak to us,
to reveal your will and give us your guidance,
but all too often when your call comes we fail to recognise it.
Though we talk of prayer being a two-way encounter,
the reality is usually different;
we seldom seriously expect to hear your voice.
Give us a readiness to be guided by the wisdom of others
so that we may recognise your voice
and understand what you are saying.
We ask it in the name of Christ.   *Nick Fawcett*

165 Living God,
you do not compel us to serve you
but you invite us rather to respond to your love.
You do not impose your will upon us
or dictate the course we should take,
but instead you offer your guidance,
giving us signposts to walk by,
yet ultimately leaving the decisions we must make in
our hands.
We thank you for this wonderful expression of trust,
this freedom to choose and discover for ourselves,
and we ask that you will help us to use it wisely,
trusting you in return,
and seeking, so far as we understand it,
to honour your will.
Give us wisdom and courage to make the right decisions,
at the right time
and in the right place,
to the glory of your name.   *Nick Fawcett*

166   Lord Jesus Christ,
we praise you for your willingness to share our humanity,
and for everything that means.
We thank you that you endured the darkness of death,
knowingly offering your life.
We rejoice that you rose again,
and that you were present once more,
leading the way to life in all its fullness.
Teach us that, whatever we may face, you will guide
our footsteps,
showing us the path we must take
and leading us safely towards your kingdom.
Lord Jesus Christ,
we praise you for that assurance,
and we put our trust in you,
this day and always.   *Nick Fawcett*

167   Sovereign God,
we cannot always make sense of life,
your purpose sometimes hard to understand
and our experiences a puzzle.
We feel frustrated when things don't work out as we hope;
confused when the way we thought you were leading us
no longer feels right;
troubled when doors that once had beckoned
suddenly seem closed firmly in our face.
We cannot be sure whether such moments are meant
to happen
or whether they run counter to your purpose,
but what we know for certain is that where one door closes
you are able to open another.
Help us, instead of regretting what has been,
to look forward to what is to come
and to be ready to grasp the future,
responding to each opportunity you give us as it comes.
In the name of Christ we ask it.   *Nick Fawcett*

168   Teach us, Lord,
      to take stock, thoughtfully, honestly and prayerfully,
      so that we may see ourselves as we really are
      rather than as we imagine ourselves to be.   *Nick Fawcett*

169   Gracious God,
      teach us not to walk unthinkingly through life
      but to reflect on all we see and experience,
      and thus glimpse your hand at work.   *Nick Fawcett*

170   Living God,
      whatever the pressures and duties of the day,
      teach us to find time for stillness,
      and, in seeing you there,
      may we see you always and everywhere,
      through the grace of Christ.   *Nick Fawcett*

171   Lord of all,
      we have made time and space for quietness to hear
      your voice.
      Go with us now into the turmoil of life,
      with all its noise and confusion,
      all its demands and responsibilities,
      and may your peace rest with us there,
      this day and for evermore.   *Nick Fawcett*

172   Sovereign God,
      in the rush and bustle of life,
      teach us to recognise the one thing worth pursuing above
      all else –
      your awesome love revealed in Christ.   *Nick Fawcett*

173   God of the still small voice,
      teach us each day to find time for moments of quietness –
      time to ponder,
      to pray and to meditate on your gracious love.
      Breathe peace within our souls,
      so that we may see the demands and responsibilities of
      daily life
      in a fresh light,

able to meet them with rekindled faith
and calm assurance,
through Jesus Christ our Lord.   *Nick Fawcett*

174 Gentle and gracious God,
calm our minds where they are troubled,
ease our bodies where they are weary,
soothe our spirits where they are in turmoil.
Teach us to find our strength in stillness and quiet
and, in the love of Christ,
to find rest for our souls.   *Nick Fawcett*

175 Gracious God,
so often we deny ourselves your blessing
through failing to turn to you;
failing to respond to your love
and to receive the mercy, joy, peace and new life
you so long to bring us.
We come now, therefore,
making time and space for you,
and opening our lives to all you would pour into them.
Teach us, as we welcome you today,
to welcome you equally every day and every moment,
until you finally welcome us into your eternal kingdom,
through Jesus Christ our Lord.   *Nick Fawcett*

176 Lord Jesus Christ,
remind us afresh today of your transforming power,
your ability to take something ordinary
and turn it into something special.
Take, then, our worship,
and, by your Spirit, make it into something beautiful to you,
bringing you glory and stirring again our hearts within us.
Take what we are,
and by your Spirit once more create us anew,
so that our lives will speak not of our weakness
but of your saving love and gracious power,
to the glory of your name.   *Nick Fawcett*

177   God of peace,
quieten our hearts
and help us to be still in your presence.
We find this so hard to do,
for our lives are full of noise and confusion,
a host of demands and responsibilities
seeming to press in upon us from every side,
consuming our time and sapping our energy.
We run here and there,
doing this and that,
always something else to think about,
another pressing matter demanding our attention –
and then suddenly,
in the middle of it all,
we stop and realise we have forgotten you,
the one we depend on to give us strength and to calm
our spirits.
God of peace,
we offer you now this little space we have made
in the frantic scramble of life.
Meet with us,
so that we may return to our daily routine with a new
perspective,
an inner tranquillity,
and a resolve to make time for you regularly
so that we may use all our time more effectively
in the service of your kingdom,
through Jesus Christ our Lord.   *Nick Fawcett*

178   Gracious God,
we thank you for this opportunity to worship you,
these few moments set aside to listen,
to reflect,
to respond.
Forgive us that such moments are all too few;
that we allow our time with you to be crowded out
by other demands on our time.
There is always something else that needs doing –
another letter to write,

another meal to prepare,
another job to finish,
another meeting to attend –
and so it goes on,
one thing after another calling for our attention
and forcing you to the back of the queue.
Gracious God, there is much that needs to be done,
but help us to understand that there is nothing as important
as spending time in your presence,
for without your strength, your peace and your
renewing touch
we lose our perspective on everything,
depriving ourselves of the resources we most need.
Help us, then, not simply to find some place for you,
but to give you pride of place,
for only then will we experience the fullness of life
you so long to give us,
through Jesus Christ our Lord.   *Nick Fawcett*

179   Lord Jesus Christ,
      time and again throughout your ministry you made time to
      be still,
      to draw away from the crowds
      so that in the quietness you could reflect on your calling.
      You needed those moments,
      just as we need them in our turn.
      So now we have made a space in our lives,
      away from the daily demands,
      away from the usual routine.
      We are here, Lord, with time for you,
      in stillness and in quietness to seek your will.
      Use these moments
      to refresh us,
      to feed us,
      to challenge and inspire us.
      Fill them with your love
      and so may we be filled to overflowing,
      by your grace.   *Nick Fawcett*

180 Loving God,
we talk of peace but all too rarely find it,
for our minds are full of a multitude of concerns,
which pull us this way and that
until we feel bewildered and confused.
We hear your still small voice bidding us to let go and rest,
but always there is another call,
another demand on our attention pressing in upon us,
and before we know it your word is drowned in the noisy
bustle of life.
We cannot ignore the world or our responsibilities within it,
and we would not want to,
for there is so much you have given us that is good,
but help us always to make time for you within it,
so that even when chaos seems to reign,
your quietness may fill our souls
bringing an inner calm that nothing will ever be able to shake.
In Christ's name we pray.   *Nick Fawcett*

181 Sovereign God,
we are here to worship you,
having made a space in our lives to pause and reflect.
We come to listen to your word,
and to ponder in the silence what you would say to us.
We come to hear your voice,
and in the stillness to receive your guidance.
Open our eyes to your presence,
our hearts to your love
and our minds to your will.
Direct our thoughts,
enlarge our understanding,
and shape our lives,
so that we may live and work for you,
to the glory of your name.   *Nick Fawcett*

182 Gracious God,
you have promised to all who love you
a peace that passes understanding.
Forgive us that we have failed to make this our own.

We rush about,
our minds preoccupied by our problems.
We brood over situations that we cannot hope to change,
magnifying them out of all proportion.
We worry about what the future may hold
instead of focusing on the present moment
and living each day as it comes.
Teach us that you hold all things in your hands
and that, even when our worries prove justified,
you will give us strength to get through.
Whatever clouds may appear on the horizon
and whatever storms life might throw against us,
may our minds be at rest,
our spirits at peace and our hearts untroubled,
through Jesus Christ our Lord.   *Nick Fawcett*

183   Living God,
in the rush and bustle of each day we all too often lose sight
of you,
our minds occupied by the responsibilities,
demands and difficulties confronting us.
Instead of turning to you,
we get sucked in ever deeper,
getting these out of all perspective
and denying ourselves the strength we need to meet them.
Teach us to find time for you,
if only for a few moments,
so that we may hear your voice and discern your will.
Teach us to step back and take stock,
so that we may then step forward,
renewed in faith, strengthened in spirit,
and equipped for whatever you may ask.
In Jesus' name we ask it.   *Nick Fawcett*

184   Living God,
too often we rush from one thing to the next,
preoccupied with the demands and responsibilities of
each day,
and wondering where we might find the strength to see
us through.

Yet instead of turning to you we struggle on as best as
we can.
Teach us to create space in our lives for you,
to make a few moments every day in which we can be quiet
and still,
and teach us to do that not as an afterthought but
instinctively,
recognising that when we give you your proper place,
everything else will fit into place as well.
In Christ's name we ask it.   *Nick Fawcett*

185   Loving God,
       in all the stress and rush of life it is so easy to forget you
       and to lose our way.
       In the press of each day,
       preoccupied with our problems, pursuits,
       plans and responsibilities
       we allow you to be crowded out.
       We strive and fret over things that cannot satisfy,
       we brood over what is unimportant,
       frantically suppressing that sense of emptiness deep within.
       Teach us to untangle ourselves from everything that
       enslaves us
       and to open our hearts afresh to you,
       so that we might find rest and nourishment for our souls
       and life in all its fullness,
       through Jesus Christ our Lord.   *Nick Fawcett*

186   Loving God,
       we live at such a hectic pace,
       our lives so busy and pressurised,
       with never a moment to spare.
       Yet so often we forget the one thing we really need:
       time to pause and ponder,
       to take stock of our lives and reflect on your goodness
       so that we might understand what it is that you would say
       to us.
       Draw near to us now in these few moments of quietness.
       Teach us to be still and to know your presence,
       through Jesus Christ our Lord.   *Nick Fawcett*

187   We pray quietly to be faithful to you, Lord God,
in good times and in bad.
May we not be fair-weather friends;
we want to love you with no conditions,
as you have loved us,
through Jesus your Son.   *Gerald O'Mahony*

188   Jesus, your mother Mary
believed in you
in success and in seeming failure and disaster.
Give us, please, the same loyal love for you
in our own life and times.   *Gerald O'Mahony*

189   May we learn to rejoice
when we get into trouble
for doing the right thing,
since that is what happened to you, Jesus. *Gerald O'Mahony*

190   May we not judge our Christian religion
by the numbers who come to church,
or our power and influence in the country.
Instead in all humility may we
continue to strive to do God's will,
no matter what the world thinks of us.   *Gerald O'Mahony*

191   After two thousand years
the Church is still struggling
against a world of unbelief.
We pray for courage, dear Jesus,
knowing that the Apostles you chose
felt the same as we do today.   *Gerald O'Mahony*

192   As your Apostle Peter himself said, dear Lord,
if we are persecuted,
let it be for doing the right thing,
not because we are guilty
of wrongdoing.   *Gerald O'Mahony*

193 Lord Jesus, we pray to understand
that if we live a good life
in imitation of you,
we may meet opposition,
and even hatred. *Gerald O'Mahony*

194 Crosses come to us when we make mistakes
and crosses come to us when we do the right thing.
Father of Jesus and our Father,
unite our crosses with his,
that we may not be alone
in our darkest hours. *Gerald O'Mahony*

195 Father of love,
if we think of you as being harsh,
then we ourselves will suffer.
May we know how generous you are
so as to become more like you. *Gerald O'Mahony*

196 Jesus, Son of God,
you are the very image of God your Father.
May we always look at you
to remind ourselves what God is like:
compassionate, encouraging,
ever-living, ever-loving. *Gerald O'Mahony*

197 Father, may our worship of you
be faithful, honest and simple.
We ask you this through the one who became a little child,
Jesus, your Son and our Lord. *Gerald O'Mahony*

198 Saint Paul asks us not to call each other names
or allow any form of spitefulness.
Loving God, teach us to show to others
the forgiveness you always show to us.
May we always speak of one another with respect,
and think the best of everyone. *Gerald O'Mahony*

199 May we not be afraid of our own weakness,
since God's forgiveness
is bigger than anything we could do wrong,
and his power works best
when we are not proud.   *Gerald O'Mahony*

200 In our hardness of heart
we are sometimes tempted
to think of God as hard-hearted.
We pray to know the joy of the real God. *Gerald O'Mahony*

201 Jesus risen came bringing the Holy Spirit
and peace.
May we bring God's peace with us
wherever we go.   *Gerald O'Mahony*

202 The prophet Job
seemed sometimes very weary with his life.
We pray for a greater awareness
of God's being with us,
and a greater trust in God's promises.   *Gerald O'Mahony*

203 God our Father,
we pray that you will always provide
for the children you yourself created,
through Christ our Lord.   *Gerald O'Mahony*

204 Lord God,
through Jesus you call on us
to become apostles of your word.
Without your grace we cannot do this;
so give us, please, the wisdom and strength we need
in the power of the Holy Spirit.   *Gerald O'Mahony*

205 'No eye has seen, nor ear heard . . .
what God has prepared for those who love him.'
May our eyes and ears be opened
to see how much you loved us first, dear God,
so that we will want
to love you in return.   *Gerald O'Mahony*

206 In our own daily worries and anxieties,
may we remember
that our Father in heaven
knows and loves every hair on our heads.
We are worth more than hundreds of sparrows.
Gerald O'Mahony

207 Jesus bids us not to be afraid,
but to speak the truths he taught us
courageously, boldly,
because they are more powerful
than the world's wisdom.   *Gerald O'Mahony*

208 May we never be afraid to ask for help,
since those who help us
will not be forgotten by Jesus:
they will most certainly
not lose their reward.   *Gerald O'Mahony*

209 We pray for all those
who find their lives too heavy,
and who fall into depression.
May they know that you do not condemn,
but that you wish
to carry their burdens with them.   *Gerald O'Mahony*

210 Dear Lord and Father of us all,
we believe that Jesus your Son
is in the same boat with us,
he who is Christ our Lord.   *Gerald O'Mahony*

211 Jesus warned us
that there would be wars and rumours of wars,
there would be earthquakes and famines.
May we listen to him as he says,
'Take heart, it is I; do not be afraid.'   *Gerald O'Mahony*

212 Father in heaven, you never did shut the door on us.
Jesus by his dying and rising showed us
that the way to you was open,
the same Jesus who reigns with you for ever.
Gerald O'Mahony

213 In Jesus we know
that death is only a sleep
from which he will wake us up again.   *Gerald O'Mahony*

214 We pray for those who have died,
especially those who are dear to us.
May not even death separate them
from the love of Christ.
May we find them again in him.   *Gerald O'Mahony*

215 Father, may the words of your Son
come to mean more to us than any other words.
Reassure us now
so that we will live life as he lived it.   *Gerald O'Mahony*

216 Resentment and anger,
these are foul things,
so the Bible tells us.
When a quarrel is brewing
may we as followers of Christ
be the first to unclench the fist.   *Gerald O'Mahony*

217 God has forgiven us already,
but we block out God's forgiveness
if we do not let it flow through us
to those people who have offended us.
We pray to let go of our resentments.   *Gerald O'Mahony*

218 'If we nurse anger against one another
how can we demand compassion from God?'
So writes a wise man from before the time of Jesus.
We pray to become compassionate,
just as God is compassionate.   *Gerald O'Mahony*

219 'Even a just person sins
seven times in the day,' so says the Bible.
The Apostle Peter was happy
to forgive a just person;
but Jesus said we must forgive everyone,
every time.   *Gerald O'Mahony*

220 Jesus, please remind us
how much we need to forgive each other
before we can know ourselves forgiven.   *Gerald O'Mahony*

221 As followers of Jesus,
we ourselves do our level best,
but we forgive those who do less well.
Teach us, dear Jesus,
that love is not a competition.   *Gerald O'Mahony*

222 Please, Holy Spirit,
give me the love to love those who need my love;
give me infectious joy;
give me patience, starting from now;
make me kind, good and generous;
keep me faithful to my promises
and forbearing with those
who find it hard to keep their promises;
keep me gentle in all circumstances;
keep your shepherd's crook firmly
in charge of me and my temper;
give me the courtesy of a knight in shining armour;
keep my moods level, neither madly hot nor too cold;
give me faithful love in married or single life.
     Gerald O'Mahony

223 We are only mirrors,
and we can only love as we are loved.
God of love, show your love to our blind eyes,
so that we will love you more generously in return.
We ask this through Jesus your Son.   *Gerald O'Mahony*

224 In silence for a few moments
we share with God our deepest longings.
These come from God,
so God is predisposed to fulfil them
in his own way, in his own time.   *Gerald O'Mahony*

225   Lord, we pray that as Christians
we may listen more attentively
and with greater urgency than ever before
to the words of Jesus;
give us more awareness of your presence with us,
both in our worship and in our daily ministry,
giving us the courage to live out your truth with joy.
Susan Sayers

226   Heavenly Father, may your words of truth
take root in our hearts and grow to rich maturity.
May we hear your will for us and act upon it;
may we take seriously our responsibility
to encourage and nurture one another in faith
at every age and every stage.   *Susan Sayers*

227   Lord, awaken in us our need of you
and make us hungry and thirsty for you,
both as individuals and as the Church of God.
Let no other issues side-track us from seeking you,
and increase our love and compassion
so that we long to serve out your love
to the world around us.   *Susan Sayers*

228   Faithful God, we pray for the gift
of deeper faith in you,
so that we trust you in a way
that alters our dependence on everything else,
and allows us clearer vision
as to the direction and role of the Church.
Remind us that it is your Church, and not ours;
your work, your power and your kingdom.   *Susan Sayers*

229   Lord, we want to pray for stronger faith
and the courage to live up to our calling;
for the grace to act always
with the generosity of spirit you show to us,
until the whole Church models the wisdom
which the world counts as foolishness.   *Susan Sayers*

230 Father, we have heard your words and your challenge
to build our lives wisely on the bedrock of faith;
may all of us who profess to be Christians
act on what we have heard.
Bless and inspire all who preach and teach the faith
and make our worship pure and holy
and acceptable to you.   *Susan Sayers*

231 God of truth, we pray that your Church
may be led into the way of truth
and an ever-deepening understanding
of your nature and your will.
We pray for our leaders and teachers and pastors;
we pray for right priorities
and a softening of the ground of our hearts.   *Susan Sayers*

232 Holy God, may the worship of your Church
throughout the world be attentive and expectant,
ready to be set on fire again and again
with the outrageous foolishness of loving,
without exceptions and without limits and without praise.
                                           Susan Sayers

233 Father, help us all in your Church
to understand what it really means to love and serve you.
At the times of testing, strengthen us,
at unexpected or undeserved suffering, support us,
at the end of our energy, revive us
and teach us through it all the inexplicable peace and joy
that comes from doing your will.   *Susan Sayers*

234 Unchanging God, change us from the heart
until the whole Church awakens to your love
that reaches out, nurtures and celebrates,
neither holding back from what is difficult,
nor rushing where angels fear to tread.
We pray for sensitivity and courage.   *Susan Sayers*

235   Loving Father, whenever we start to get offended
      by your generosity or open-mindedness,
      give us the grace to repent and join your rejoicing.
      Guard the Church against self-righteousness
      and all rules and limits which you would not own,
      but keep always before us the rule of love.   *Susan Sayers*

236   Lord, we thank you for all the help and encouragement
      we are given from the Church –
      from its worship, teaching and fellowship;
      from its faithfulness in prayer.
      Bless and further all loving ministry
      in word and sacrament throughout the world Church;
      inspire us all to want your will and to do it.   *Susan Sayers*

237   Loving God, guide your Church
      into ways of spiritual beauty and gracious wisdom.
      May your word be spoken out with passion
      and heard with humility and joy.
      Sustain and feed us so that we bear fruit in abundance.
                                                Susan Sayers

238   Father, when either the traditional or the progressive
      blinds us to the truth of your will,
      clear our vision and speak through our prejudices
      until we are once again open to your changing.
      May we be, before anything else, your people,
      sharing your concerns and desires.   *Susan Sayers*

239   Lord of all, give your Church such maturity and wisdom
      that we may not be swayed from our purpose and calling
      by trivialities or worldly pressures,
      but know increasingly our dependence
      on you in all things and proclaim your gospel
      with steadfastness and joy.   *Susan Sayers*

240   Stop us, dear God,
      from rushing in where angels fear to tread.
      Rebuke our headstrong ways.
      Deflect us from foolhardy paths.
      Alert us to meet a crisis that requires us to be prepared.
                                              Ray Simpson

241 Help us to grow today
in understanding and sensitivity,
in patience and prayerfulness. *Ray Simpson*

242 Good God,
from you flows all goodness, all light.
Help us to discern goodness wherever it surfaces
and to make common cause with it,
for you are the Father of light. *Ray Simpson*

243 Universal God, you have a plan
for every person
and for every situation in the world.
But we are so dim.
We are so deaf.
Help us to become God-guided instruments
and always to be in just the place you wish us to be.
Ray Simpson

244 Teach me when to be silent and when to speak,
when to listen and when to leave,
when to praise and when to refrain,
when to laugh and when to weigh,
when to tell and when to wait. *Ray Simpson*

245 High King of the universe,
we offer you our possessions.
Make them all your own.
We offer you our mindsets
and we place them at your feet.
May we be filled with your Presence
as incense fills a holy place.
We offer you the shadows of our lives,
the things that are crushed,
our little deaths and our final death.
May these be like the straw in the out-stable.
May something beautiful for you
be born in all this straw. *Ray Simpson*

246   Thank you, Lord,
        that even if we are difficult or blinkered people,
        you can put holy desires into our hearts
        and divine intimations before our eyes,
        so that we come through obstacles
        to our eternal resurrection.   *Ray Simpson*

247   Lord, grant me the strength to do without things.
        Grant me the wisdom to see the 'within' of things.
        Grant me the knowledge to take the measure of evil spirits.
        Grant me understanding to know you who alone are true.
                                                        Ray Simpson

248   Infinite One of the wise heart,
        Saving One of the clear sight,
        Knowing One of the hidden deeps,
        may I learn from you as an eager pupil,
        may I learn from life as a humble child,
        may I learn from night, may I learn from day,
        may I learn from soul friends, may I learn from stillness.
                                                        Ray Simpson

249   All-seeing God,
        who has given to us the holy Scriptures,
        help us so to value them,
        to read, mark, learn and inwardly digest them,
        that we may grow in wisdom
        and in understanding of your ways,
        now and for eternity.   *Ray Simpson*

250   Eternal Word of God,
        whose Spirit moves prophets, recordists and readers,
        give us discernment of spirits
        and help us understand every part of Scripture
        in the light of the True Way.   *Ray Simpson*

251   Lord, you remember us
        and know our every thought.
        Help us to remember you
        and know your words to us.   *Ray Simpson*

252 Risen Christ, as we read this passage,
may we be aware that you are here with us.
Eternal truth flows through the words we read.
You know the particular word
that we most need now.
We open ourselves to you.
Please speak to us. *Ray Simpson*

253 Make us sensitive, Lord,
to your tones, your style, your feelings
as we recall your work in Bible times.
Re-envision us.
Recharge us.
May we touch the earth that you touched.
May you touch the earth
upon which we stand today. *Ray Simpson*

254 Make us attentive to your clear commands.
Make us attentive to the sighing of your world.
Make us attentive to your whispering tones.
Make us attentive to your slightest wish. *Ray Simpson*

255 Eternal Truth,
grant us humility to know how little we know.
Give us clarity to know what is best for us to learn.
Show us a good way to this.
Form us in the art of asking useful questions.
Help us grow, like Jesus, in understanding. *Ray Simpson*

256 Christ of fearless love,
take us to our point of greatest weakness
and let us find you there.
May your strength
be made complete in our frailty. *Ray Simpson*

257 Holy, True and Real One,
help us to be true, help us to be real.
Help us to know our own mind.
Help us to know what we must say 'Yes' to
and what we must say 'No' to.
May our lives be like a blank sheet of paper. *Ray Simpson*

258 Pardoner and Restorer,
help us to listen,
without judgement and with empathy,
to the stories of those who are inflamed.
Help us to stay calm and learn what we can.
Help us to be clear about what we can achieve,
not to promise what we cannot deliver
and to take responsibility for what we can deliver.
If it is possible, help us to walk a mile
in the other's shoes and even to want the best for them,
as for us.   *Ray Simpson*

259 We pray for an end to the injustices
which become breeding grounds of war.
We pray for the restoration of fellowship
and the building of integrity.
We pray for commitment
to the unending struggle against selfish ways
and violation of human dignity.
We pray for that peace
which is the full blossoming of our life together.
                                                   Ray Simpson

260 Lord, the nations rage
and people around us become vengeful.
You see it all.
The kingdoms of this world
will become your kingdom.
So help us look upon what is happening
with the calm assurance and quiet confidence
of the Risen Christ,
and leave the rest to you.   *Ray Simpson*

261 You who order the universe,
pour your oil on the troubled waters of our lives.
We bring to you the troubles
in our places of work,
in our relationships,
in our church
and in the world.
Calm us, and help us rest in you.   *Ray Simpson*

262   Boundless Nourisher,
help me to retreat in order to advance;
to move out of tram lines and
reorientate my life with you.
Help me to relax and listen,
to observe and receive;
perhaps to walk in the steps of saints,
or to read and reflect and renew my mind.
Above all, may I stop running away,
and learn to wonder as I wander with you.   *Ray Simpson*

263   I will come apart with you, Lord,
that you may still my heart.
I will come apart with you, Lord,
that you may stock my mind.
I will come apart with you, Lord,
that you may steel my will.
I will retreat with you, Lord,
that together we may advance.   *Ray Simpson*

264   Lead me, Lord, into a place of prayer,
to live simply, silently and alone with you,
so that I may die to myself quicker
and Christ may grow in me faster;
so that you may give more of him
to the world that hungers for him.
Echoes words of Catherine Doherty   *Ray Simpson*

265   You, Lord, burn in this place.
Your presence fills it.
Strip from me all that is not of you.
Call me to whatever you will.
Lead me wherever you will.   *Ray Simpson*

266   God, make my heart a little cell.
Keep harm without, keep peace within.
God, make my heart an altar
where I may gaze into your face.
God, make my heart your home
where I am content to be with you.   *Ray Simpson*